THOUGHTS OF
POWER AND LOVE

D0770106

BOOKS and AUDIOCASSETTES by
SUSAN JEFFERS, PH.D.

Books

Dare to Connect
Feel the Fear and Do It Anyway
The Journey from Lost to Found
Opening Our Hearts to Men

The "Fear Less" Series
Inner Talk for a Confident Day
Inner Talk for a Love that Works
Inner Talk for Peace of Mind

Audiocassettes

The Art of Fearbusting
Dare to Connect (Book-on-Tape)
A Fearbusting Workshop
Feel the Fear and Do It Anyway
    (Book-on-Tape—also comes in
    abridged version)
Flirting from the Heart
Opening Our Hearts to Each Other
Opening Our Hearts to Men
    (Book-on-Tape)

The "Fear Less" Audio Series
Inner Talk for a Confident Day
Inner Talk for a Love that Works
Inner Talk for Peace of Mind

Available at your local bookstore, or call

(800) 654-5126

THOUGHTS OF POWER AND LOVE

Susan Jeffers, Ph.D.

Hay House, Inc.
Carson, CA

Copyright © 1995 by Susan Jeffers

Published and distributed in the United States by: Hay House, Inc.
1154 E. Dominguez St., P.O. Box 6204, Carson, CA 90749-6204

Edited by: Jill Kramer
Designed by: ATLIS Graphics and Design, Mechanicsburg, PA

All rights reserved. No part of this book may be reproduced by any mechanical,
photographic, or electronic process, or in the form of a phonographic recording, nor
may it be stored in a retrieval system, transmitted, or otherwise be copied for public
or private use–other than for "fair use" as brief quotations embodied in articles and
reviews without prior written permission of the publisher.

Library of Congress Cataloging-in-Publication Data

Jeffers, Susan J., date.
Thoughts of power and love / Susan Jeffers.
     p.   cm.
  ISBN 1-56170-122-X (trd. paper)
   1. Love—Quotations, maxims, etc.   2. Self-actualization
(Psychology)—Quotations, maxims, etc.   I. Title.
BF575.L8J46   1994
152.4'1—dc20   94-38171
                                  CIP

ISBN 1-56170-122-X

99 98 97 96 95   5 4 3 2 1
First Printing, November 1994

Printed in the United States of America

To my beloved husband,
Mark Shelmerdine,
who is the perfect embodiment
of power and love...

What a combination!

CONTENTS

Introduction . . . . *vii*

I   No Need for Walls 1

II   The World Is Filled with Lovers! 27

III   Rising in Love 47

IV   From Victim to Creator 69

V   Say YES! to You 95

VI   Not to Worry 111

VII   It's All Happening Perfectly 139

VIII Higher and Higher .157

IX   There's Always More 177

X   You Are the World .197

INTRODUCTION

I am so thankful to the wonderful people at Hay House for making *Thoughts of Power and Love* possible. Creating a quote book was a great privilege for me. The reason is...I love quote books! I read them all the time! I buy them for family and friends!

The reason I love them as much as I do is that often a simple quote has changed my whole perspective on life, or given me courage where there had been only fear, or shown me where I had been looking for answers in all the wrong places. It is my fervent wish that some of the quotes in this book will do the same for you.

The thoughts presented within come from ideas discussed in all of my books, tapes, workshops, and public speaking appearances...but more significantly, they come from fascinating insights I've had as I've journeyed through my own life. Since there really are no strangers, most of my observations will apply to your life as well.

If you come upon a quote that you don't agree with, just let it go. If you come upon a quote that touches you, write it on a little card and put it on your desk or mirror or anyplace you can easily see it. Look at it often. It takes consciousness to break old habits of being, doing, and feeling...and quotes do a beautiful job of keeping us conscious! They point the way toward a life filled with joy, abundance, power, and love...all of which I wish for you.

From my heart to yours.

Susan Jeffers, Ph.D.

NO NEED
FOR WALLS

I

NO NEED
FOR WALLS

If the sign on your heart says "WELCOME," the love will come pouring in from everywhere!

When we build walls around our Heart, we create our own isolation. We separate ourselves from all that is truly beautiful in this world.

NO NEED
FOR WALLS

We come into this world connected with one another on a very deep level. Even though our training is about competing, our Souls are about embracing.

———————❀———————

When we depend on the world to invite us in, we are always on the outside looking in, yearning to be in someone else's circle of being.

NO NEED
FOR WALLS

It's important for us to create our own circle of being into which we can invite others. That way, we never feel excluded.

Many people sit at home wondering why they are so alone. Sitting at home **guarantees** being alone!

When we are friendly, we meet the nicest people!

Connection is made easier when we approach other people with the purpose of making **THEM** feel better about themselves. Usually, our purpose is to make a good impression so that **WE** can feel better about ourselves!

NO NEED
FOR WALLS

A not-so-good reason to reach out to others: To "fix" something within ourselves.

A good reason to reach out to others: To share our warmth and caring and love.

If you are a "nice guy" because of the joy of being a giving person, that's great; but if you are a "nice guy" only because you're desperate for approval, that's not so great. **Love can't flow from desperation.**

Impression-making is truly the sad arena of "empty suits."

NO NEED
FOR WALLS

When we focus only on the external packaging—ours or anyone else's—alienation prevails. Connection requires an inward look.

———❖———

When we allow external trappings to be the measure of our Self-worth, **instead of feeling like a somebody, we end up feeling like a nobody!** We lose sight of who we truly could be—loving, caring, and sharing—and wonder why we feel empty inside.

If you want to drive yourself crazy, try to figure out what other people want you to be. And then try to become it. A perfect recipe for Self-destruction!

———❈———

Our three biggest barriers to meaningful connection—low Self-worth, dependency, and fear—have nothing to do with anyone "out there."

NO NEED
FOR WALLS

When we are lost to ourselves, how can we possibly connect meaningfully with someone else?

———❖———

"Lost people" are needy. They attract and are attracted to the unhealthiest people! When the neediness is gone, a much healthier group of people shows up!

Rejection never feels good. But it certainly hurts less when we are not needing something from the person who is rejecting us!

Ultimately, we learn: When we approach someone lovingly and are treated unkindly, we are face to face with **THEIR** insecurities. Their behavior has nothing to do with us...even though **our own insecurities make us believe that it does!**

NO NEED
FOR WALLS

Secure people don't treat other people unkindly, no matter what the situation.

———————✹———————

When anyone puts you down for being who you truly are, it is your signal to move on to others who applaud you for being who you truly are.

NO NEED
FOR WALLS

Emblazon this thought on your mind: **NO MATTER WHAT RESPONSE YOU GET FROM ANYONE YOU MEET, YOU ARE A WORTHWHILE PERSON!**

Your worth depends only on what **YOU** think of you! Sometimes that's the problem!

NO NEED
FOR WALLS

Everyone in your life is a "practice person."
How you **react** to them allows you to see
what you have to work on within yourself.

The ability to connect has to do with
healing our inner wounds and increasing
our Self-respect.

NO NEED
FOR WALLS

As we heal our inner pain, we begin to notice the beauty of all those people who would welcome our love. And in this wholesome space, loving connections can occur in all areas of our lives.

NO NEED
FOR WALLS

When we have thoughts of competing, controlling, and comparing, we are led straight to hell. When we have thoughts about caring, sharing, and loving, we are led straight to Heaven. **And you thought you had to die to go to Heaven!**

By realizing that every "stranger" in that crowded room would love to feel cared about and is just as fearful of rejection as we are, we are in harmony with them even before we ever say hello.

NO NEED
FOR WALLS

How do you carry yourself? Walk, sit, and stand tall, delighted that you are who you are!

What do you say? Be interested instead of interesting!

NO NEED
FOR WALLS

Drink in the beauty of friendship! In this
world of constant change, we need the
comfort of friendship more than ever before.

It is important to include in our circle those
with whom we can authentically share,
Heart and Soul, all that we hold inside.
There is never a need to feel alone in
this world.

NO NEED
FOR WALLS

Intimacy is the feeling we get when we mutually open our minds and hearts in total acceptance of each other to truly hear what the other is saying and feel what the other is feeling. At its best, it is the sense of human connection at the level of the Soul.

❖

When we open up, others will open up. In sharing, we offer a safe space for inner truths to be told.

NO NEED
FOR WALLS

Sharing who we are makes the walls of separation come tumbling down.

———————❖———————

When we finally learn to open up, we find that what we hold inside is nothing to be ashamed of, rather, it is wonderfully human!

NO NEED
FOR WALLS

When we are blind to the beauty in others, we are obviously blind to the beauty in ourselves.

As we open our hearts to others, we begin to discover the truth of our own inner beauty, inner strength, and inner light.

NO NEED
FOR WALLS

As we acknowledge our inner beauty, we begin to walk tall and take pride in who we are as human beings.

As our hearts become filled with light, we automatically project this light into a very dark and unloving world. And as a lamp brings light into a room, our "lamp" brings light into the world around us.

NO NEED
FOR WALLS

———————————

Visualize a healing light pouring forth
from every pore of your body and touching
everyone you meet. When we project our
light onto other beings, we tap into the
essence of connection.

———— ❋ ————

Projecting imaginary light into any room
immediately makes it a brighter, warmer
room. It helps to melt the ice around people's
hearts, especially your own!

"I GREET THE LIGHT IN YOU" is the thought that opens your heart and allows you to see beyond the darkness.

———◆———

Consider this: The more light you see in other human beings, by definition, the brighter your world becomes.

NO NEED
FOR WALLS

It is only when we know there is a
light that shines within each of us, even
though it may be badly dimmed by life's
experiences, that the circle of connection
is truly possible.

THE WORLD IS FILLED WITH LOVERS!

II

THE WORLD IS
FILLED WITH LOVERS!

No scarcity here! From the Soul's perspective, lovers abound!

———————— ✦ ————————

This is not a "one drink of water in the desert" kind of world. There are so many people to love.

THE WORLD IS
FILLED WITH LOVERS!

If you are not in a successful relationship, the likelihood is...your type is not your type!

Surprise! The perfect partner for you may be nothing like you ever imagined him or her to be!

THE WORLD IS
FILLED WITH LOVERS!

What many of us find attractive in a mate is inconsistent with what we say we want our mate to be, hence, inconsistent with what we say we want to be. It's time we make up our minds!

A simple trick for finding a perfect match: Be yourself and see who shows up!

THE WORLD IS
FILLED WITH LOVERS!

It's not only about who you are attracted to.
It's also about who is attracted to the truth of
who you are.

While we may blame others for our inability
to connect romantically, we would do better
to look at some of the "uncoupling" beliefs
we hold inside.

THE WORLD IS
FILLED WITH LOVERS!

When you honor the essence of who you truly are and proudly let your light shine through, your chances for a successful "match" are greatly increased.

———————✿———————

Some say you have to lower your standards in order to find a mate. I disagree. You need to change your focus from outer trappings to inner power and love. **That's raising your standards!**

THE WORLD IS
FILLED WITH LOVERS!

In order to find love, we need to heal those
hurts within ourselves that create barriers
to loving.

———————— ❖ ————————

When we keep our eyes open, each
relationship, positive or negative, brings us
closer and closer to the "look" of real love.

THE WORLD IS
FILLED WITH LOVERS!

When it comes to romantic love, I don't believe age should be an issue. Who are we to judge how people should or shouldn't find love?

The mirror is a great judge as to whether we would fill our own requirements in a mate. **Do our eyes reflect a loving heart?**

THE WORLD IS FILLED WITH LOVERS!

Don't believe the advertisements. Love has nothing to do with looks! It has to do with the invisible qualities of love and caring. Trust me on this one!

———— ❖ ————

The more love we project, the more loving people we will attract. Guess what we attract when we project neediness, judgment, or any of those other love-destroying qualities?

THE WORLD IS
FILLED WITH LOVERS!

Make a list of all those characteristics you would like to find in a mate…and then begin developing them in yourself!

Like attracts like! Become what you want to attract!

THE WORLD IS
FILLED WITH LOVERS!

Don't trust body language. Insecurity
sometimes makes people turn away from
those to whom they are **most** attracted!

———— ❖ ————

If you are always rejected, it is a clear signal
that you have much work to do on loving
yourself.

THE WORLD IS
FILLED WITH LOVERS!

Whether your heart is open or closed is evident to those around us. Closed hearts push people away.

⸻ ❖ ⸻

Loneliness is often the result of a closed heart. It signals we need to find the key to opening it.

THE WORLD IS FILLED WITH LOVERS!

When the door to the heart opens, we find what we've been looking for...ourselves! And we need never feel lonely again.

❈

Strangely, learning how to be alone is an important step in learning to heal our loneliness.

THE WORLD IS
FILLED WITH LOVERS!

What often looks like love is not—it is **need**.

When your neediness comes to the fore, others are smart to run the other way. Needy people can't love people; they can only use them.

THE WORLD IS
FILLED WITH LOVERS!

The cure for neediness is the creation of a life so rich that the absence of any part of it doesn't wipe us out.

———❖———

Once we can answer our own cry for help, we need never feel fearful again.

THE WORLD IS
FILLED WITH LOVERS!

In order to love others, it is essential that we love ourselves. It's all part of the same package!

Unless we end the war between the sexes, a healthy relationship between a man and woman is virtually impossible. One is seldom loving to the enemy!

THE WORLD IS FILLED WITH LOVERS!

Until both men and women feel good about themselves, they will continue to hurt each other. That's just the way it is.

I don't care what the surface behavior looks like; underneath, everyone wants to love and be loved.

THE WORLD IS
FILLED WITH LOVERS!

Equality is nothing without responsibility.
Are you ready to be responsible?

When we let go of our victim mentality
about members of the opposite sex, we open
our hearts to each other and find wonderful
people to love.

What a valuable resource men and women provide each other! When we love and learn from one another, we have a chance at wholeness.

Men and women are in a transition period. Transition, by definition, brings with it confusion. But soon the "new" becomes the "norm." **Make the "new" about love, not anger and hate!**

THE WORLD IS
FILLED WITH LOVERS!

When love becomes the "norm," we will see men and women working together to create a world that truly works for everyone.

As we truly take responsibility for our lives and honor who we are, a new dawn of love, caring, and sharing will begin.

RISING
IN LOVE

III

RISING
IN LOVE

Don't fall in love...rise in love!

We must get rid of those fairy tale expectations. Don't you know that if Romeo and Juliet had lived, their incredible neediness would have surely broken up the relationship!

Fairy tale expectations create hearts that can easily be broken.

Don't wait until you hear bells ringing. Ringing in your ears means you need to see a doctor!

RISING
IN LOVE

Passionate attachments have nothing to do with meaningful love. Real passion doesn't come from attachment; it comes from the discovery of the divine within us all.

———❖———

It is far better to allow the sexual attraction to flow from the beauty of an evolving relationship than to experience an instant attraction that quickly dissolves into disappointment and heartbreak.

Relationships are the greatest workshops going. We learn **exactly** what we haven't resolved in our own lives.

———— ❖ ————

All negative emotions are always appropriate. It is our responses to them that often are not.

RISING
IN LOVE

The only purpose of a relationship is to learn how to become a more loving person. End of story!

❖

I know of no better way to create a loving relationship than to eliminate your negative judgments. Focus only on the gifts you bring each other, and love will bloom.

Clearly, when we are judgmental—of ourselves or others—we lose our joy and lightness, qualities that come from seeing with loving eyes, not hostile ones.

———❖———

If you want to be appreciated, appreciate. If you want to be touched, touch. If you want to be loved, love. What are you waiting for?

RISING
IN LOVE

Those who constantly need to be right are, in truth, fighting a battle with a part of themselves that feels very inferior and unsure of itself. And it follows, the more self-righteous, the bigger the battle within!

There is only one time when it is absolutely appropriate for you to have the last word. That is when the last "word" happens to be "I love you!"

In relationships, we are often truthful, but
not always honest about our motivations for
being truthful! We must ask ourselves, "Do
we want to hurt, or do we want to heal?"

Being responsible for your mouth is part of
being responsible for your life!

RISING
IN LOVE

How can we have self-respect when we are constantly putting others down?

———◆———

Kids will be kids...and we forgive. Adults will be kids as well. We all need to forgive when those we love act in childlike ways.

"I love you" means very little if you are
not being a loving person to the person to
whom you are saying "I love you!"

———————

Stop playing games and losing your Soul
just so you can keep someone in your life.

RISING
IN LOVE

The toughest habit to break is dependency.
We expect someone to carry our burden,
and we call it love.

The problem with needy people is that they
can't take in anything around them. Then
they wonder why they are starving.

Isn't it strange that the less you need someone, the more you are able to love them?

———❖———

Be high on love, but not on attachment.

RISING
IN LOVE

We become very lopsided individuals
when we give up half of who we are.
Good relationships require whole people.

When we cling to another, we lose
ourselves and become their person. When
we let go, we find ourselves and become our
own person. Only then is love possible.

Dependency needs always surface in relationships. Do we choose to grow up, or do we choose to remain children?

Rejection is always a possibility in love. But when your life is rich, the loss of a love will never wipe you out.

RISING
IN LOVE

It serves the purpose of love to focus on the essence of it and not the petty details.

———————✦———————

Love in its highest form means being able to let go and allow your mate to learn and grow in whatever way he or she has to…as you must.

Use negative feelings as keys to self-discovery, not as a way to put your mate down.

❖

One of the most precious gifts we can give to those we love is to let them know that they're okay in our book.

RISING
IN LOVE

Our anger is usually about the actions **WE**
are not taking to correct the matter at hand!

The "not enough" syndrome signifies
that we have not learned to take in the
abundance that surrounds us. Abundance is
always there…in some form or another.

When we focus on abundance, we can be much more loving in our relationships. We stop collecting injustices and begin counting blessings instead.

———◆———

It enhances our self-esteem to enhance someone else's!

RISING
IN LOVE

We're all lovers-in-training...and we won't always get it right. That's reassuring!

———————✦———————

When we learn from all our relationships, how can there be any such thing as a bad relationship?

It's easy to sculpt a loving relationship.
Just cut away everything that doesn't look
like love!

In order to keep love alive, we must
consciously feed it all the magnificence we
can muster.

RISING
IN LOVE

Every day, we must ask ourselves, "How can I express my love today?" Remember that all things that are left unattended deteriorate.

When we put conscious intention into love, we create a chain reaction that keeps love growing and growing and growing.

FROM VICTIM
TO CREATOR

VI

FROM VICTIM
TO CREATOR

Do you think the world is loving? Or, do you think it's hostile? You'll create whatever you think it is.

If you think the world will treat you badly, you immerse yourself in darkness. If you think the world will embrace you lovingly, you open the doors to the light.

When you allow your internal negativity to blind you to the power and love you hold inside, you become a beggar in disguise.

———※———

Pick up the mirror instead of the magnifying glass—not to blame yourself, but to empower yourself.

FROM VICTIM
TO CREATOR

The very act of picking up the mirror
instead of the magnifying glass can be
considered one of the most loving things
that we can do for ourselves. It says to us,
"Hey, Honey, over here, where you can do
something about it! Not over there where
you can't!"

FROM VICTIM
TO CREATOR

Stop trying to figure out why someone else acts the way he or she does. The powerful question is: "Why do I react the way I do?"

———————❖———————

It's time to begin sculpting our own lives. Why give anyone but ourselves the power to shape who we are?

FROM VICTIM
TO CREATOR

The ideal shape of our lives comes from a deep inner knowing. We must take the time to listen.

———————— ❖ ————————

There is no need to wait for anyone to give you anything in your life. You have the power to create exactly what you need.

In every situation, there are a multitude of choices. Ask yourself which would contribute most to your aliveness and growth. Choose that one!

Taking responsibility means never blaming anyone else for anything you are being, doing, having, or feeling. Ouch!

FROM VICTIM
TO CREATOR

Taking responsibility means not blaming yourself! **Anything** that takes away your power or your pleasure makes you a victim. Don't make yourself a victim of yourself!

There's enough abuse in the world. There is **never** any need to beat yourself up!

Yes, you create your own unhappiness, but self-blame isn't the answer. Creating your own happiness is!

The realization that "we are doing it to ourselves" is our biggest blessing. **If we know we can create our own misery, it stands to reason we can also create our own joy.** What power!

77

FROM VICTIM
TO CREATOR

It is so convenient to blame others when we are consciously or unconsciously run by our fears.

—————❖—————

While our tendency is to resist our own responsibility in the matter, our power lies in changing what doesn't work.

Look inside. Taking responsibility means
being aware of where and when you are **not**
taking responsibility so that you can
eventually change it!

———❖———

Taking responsibility for your own
happiness increases your ability to handle
the pain and fear in your life.

FROM VICTIM
TO CREATOR

When you finally understand that you, and
no one else, create what goes on in your
head, you will, at last, be in control of your
experiences of life.

———◆———

**Blame is a powerless act! Why give away
all your power?**

FROM VICTIM
TO CREATOR

You don't have to hang out with enemies, even if they are within yourself! Learn how to move to a more loving part of your being.

When you finally take responsibility for your life, the bottomless pit of helplessness becomes filled up with power and love.

FROM VICTIM
TO CREATOR

We can't blame anyone for walking all over us. We can only notice that we are not moving out of the way! Aha!

———✦———

Remember: When we act second-class, we are treated second-class!

FROM VICTIM
TO CREATOR

When we take responsibility for moving out of the way of those who try to hurt us, we can begin to open our hearts and see the pain that lies within their hearts.

———❖———

As long as "They did it to me" remains part of our thinking, we will remain children all of our lives. It's time to grow up.

FROM VICTIM
TO CREATOR

Even if they **did** do it to us, what are **we** going to do now? "Stand tall and walk forward with our lives" is the most powerful answer.

FROM VICTIM
TO CREATOR

Stop feeling sorry for yourself. **We all come from dysfunctional families**! Why? Because our society is dysfunctional! It avoids the essence and embraces the shadow. It's never too late to turn that around!

It kills our sense of self-worth to hurt other people with our anger.

FROM VICTIM
TO CREATOR

We all have the power to find the Path that
teaches us, strengthens us, and allows us to
move away from the people and situations
that hurt us.

If you need drama in your life, move away
from victim-drama to creator-drama. The
former is filled with heartache; the latter
is filled with bliss.

Stop waiting for someone to give you your life. You'll be waiting a long time.

You have many choices in life. Always choose the Path that contributes to your growth and that makes you feel at peace with yourself and others.

FROM VICTIM
TO CREATOR

We struggle to stop struggling! There's something wrong with that scenario!

Ask yourself, "Is this action moving me to a more powerful place?" If it isn't, think twice before doing it.

FROM VICTIM
TO CREATOR

To move ahead requires that we not only let go of our own anger, but that we distance ourselves from others who are angry, and who have made themselves victims of their own beliefs.

❖

Most of us are not aware that we belong to the "moan and groan society" until we stop moaning and groaning.

FROM VICTIM
TO CREATOR

Complaint buddies help us become the worst that we could be. True friends help us become the best that we can be.

Complaint buddies offer only a continuation of our misery. True friends point us in the direction of power and healing.

When we support each other's "victim act," we become enemies to one another.

Friends are the mirror reflecting the truth of who we are.

FROM VICTIM
TO CREATOR

Walk away from friends who hurt you...
and their buying into your victim mentality
is very hurtful indeed!

If your friends constantly complain, the
solution is simple...find new friends. Don't
feel disloyal. They'll have no problem
finding someone else to complain to.

We can't control the world, but we can
control our reactions to it.

———❖———

Let's all stop playing the role of "Poor Me"
and create a new model for ourselves—that
of powerful, loving, imaginative, and
abundant adults.

FROM VICTIM
TO CREATOR

Once we get off the victim routine, it's amazing how creative we can become. We begin to pull up our power and fill ourselves with enthusiasm and a sense of wonder at the huge number of possibilities.

SAY YES!
TO YOU!

V

Remove those imaginary "Please like me" stickers from your forehead and, instead, place them in the only place they will do any good…on your mirror!

———— ✦ ————

Stop trying to be perfect. Even the Buddha had his days!

The loveliest thing you can do for yourself is to embrace the beauty of your humanness.

———————— ❖ ————————

It is through your humanness, not your perfection, that the poignant bonds of connection are finally formed.

SAY YES!
TO YOU!

Trying to be perfect is very limiting. It also creates an intense feeling of being trapped!

———※———

We go about our lives pulling ourselves down instead of building ourselves up. Maybe we should all walk around with compasses.

Change requires constant practice and repetition. Don't dwell on setbacks when they occur (and they will!); rather, focus on **every** little sign of progress.

———◈———

Nothing is as satisfying as those moments of breakthrough when you discover something about yourself that adds another piece to the jigsaw puzzle of life. The joy of discovery is delicious!

**SAY YES!
TO YOU!**

If you ever find the voice of impatience creeping in, just keep repeating to yourself: **ONE STEP AT A TIME IS ENOUGH FOR ME.**

Impatience is simply a way of beating yourself up. What's the rush?

Be patient. The world doesn't change overnight…nor do we.

———◆———

There is no quick fix. Sorry about that! But there is a cornucopia of tools to be used and mastered throughout a lifetime.

SAY YES!
TO YOU!

There is magic in the aging process. The young so rarely understand what age allows us to know. **Why would anyone resist getting older?**

———❖———

Aging allows us to drop the baggage. It is only through many life experiences that our incredible power can be brought forward in all its glory.

It's not about how far we have to go…it's about how far we have come. The older we get, the farther we've come!

———◈———

There is plenty of time. And despite what the chatter in your mind (or anyone else's) is telling you, it's all unfolding perfectly.

Practice gives you a definite advantage.
Nothing is going to "take" until you take it.

———————— ❖ ————————

LIGHTEN UP! If you have ever been
around a person who really has it together,
you are struck by their humor and ability to
laugh at themselves.

Act-as-if you really count. The difference between the way we operate in this world when we know we count and when we don't know we count is staggering!

———— ❖ ————

Loving acts raise you to the level of a magnificent being. If you don't feel good about yourself, create some loving acts.

When we attack others, we deny our oneness with humanity. Hence, in attacking others, we kill a part of ourselves.

I believe our craving in life is not to be loved but to love…ourselves and others.

We must learn to transcend the pettiness of the ego and move into a higher plane if we want to create love in our lives. The ego makes us doubt ourselves…and, therefore, makes us doubt others.

———————❖———————

To be free is simply to act on one's truth… and to allow no one else to obscure that truth.

Go slow. Trying to do too much at one time is a self-defeating mechanism that guarantees failure. Does that sound familiar?

If you make anything external the purpose of your life, you will always make yourself a candidate for mental torture. Even if you succeed in getting what you want, you will always live with the fear of losing it.

Boredom simply means that we are waiting for someone else to create excitement in our lives. How boring!

———— ❖ ————

Stand tall, take charge of your life, and honor who you are. This is a great formula for getting rid of anger!

SAY YES!
TO YOU!

The answer to honoring the Self is to figure out what you really want and then live your life accordingly.

———◆———

As long as you can remember that life is an ongoing process of learning, you won't have the disgruntling sense that you haven't made it yet.

NOT TO WORRY

VI

NOT TO
WORRY

I'LL HANDLE IT! Three of the most powerful words in the world!

———— ❖ ————

If you knew you could handle anything that came your way, what would you possibly have to fear? The answer is: **NOTHING!**

———————

The key to diminishing your fear is to develop more trust in your ability to handle whatever comes your way!

———————❖———————

Security is not having things, it's handling things!

NOT TO
WORRY

The only thing we can safely trust is our ability to handle whatever anyone says or does to us. And we can learn to handle anything!

Why are we afraid? Have you ever heard a parent calling out to a child going off to school, "Take some risks today, Darling." Considering how many "be carefuls" our parents bombarded us with, it's amazing we even manage to walk out the front door!

———❖———

NOT TO
WORRY

All of us have fear…particularly if we are growing. It comes with the territory.

———— ✦ ————

Even if it seems frightening…SO WHAT! Fear and action aren't mutually exclusive!

FEEL THE FEAR AND DO IT ANYWAY!

With each step forward, we learn to hold
fear from a position of power instead of pain.

NOT TO
WORRY

Pushing through fear is less frightening than living with the bigger underlying fear that comes from a feeling of helplessness!

———◈———

The way you get rid of the fear of doing something is to go out and do it!

Action helps us move out of helplessness and into power.

———※———

Let go of the outcome...and there is nothing to fear.

NOT TO
WORRY

You're not a failure if you don't make it; you're a success because you try!

There is no such thing as a false start if you are seriously committed to following the path of growth. Each step along the way shows you the way to where you **really** are supposed to be going. It may be a destination you never even considered!

Take time to think about what you really want in life…not what others would have you want.

"What do I want?" is a question we need to ask ourselves constantly. Wants change as we learn to find the power and love within.

NOT TO
WORRY

Allow yourself confusion as you walk through life. It is our way of sorting things out. It is through confusion that we finally come to clarity.

———✵———

When you can find the good in any decision you make, it's much easier to accept the responsibility for making it!

Don't protect, correct! The trick in life is not to worry about being off course in life; it's knowing when to correct.

———❖———

What power! In every situation there are at least 30 ways to change your point of view! There is never any need to get stuck in your perceptions.

NOT TO WORRY

Just change your attitudes, and the world changes around you.

It's impossible to make a mistake. Each decision is simply another opportunity to learn…despite the outcome.

If you haven't made any "mistakes" lately, you must be doing something wrong!

———— ✦ ————

With no mistakes, you are taking no risks! Nor are you enjoying the "goodies" life has to offer. What a waste!

NOT TO
WORRY

We need to stop worrying about making mistakes. If we are **not** making mistakes, it means we are not learning or growing.

We are not going to succeed in everything we attempt in life. That's a guarantee. In fact, the more we do in life, the more chance there is **not** to succeed in some things. But what a rich life we are having! Win or lose, we just keep winning!

We are not going to succeed in everything we attempt in life. What a relief! That's one expectation we can let go of.

———◆———

We are all designed to use our inherent power. When we don't, we experience helplessness, paralysis, and depression. Doesn't it make sense to get in touch with your power as soon as possible?

NOT TO
WORRY

When you put loving thoughts and behavior into the world, you plant seeds of self-respect. When you put unloving thoughts and behavior into the world, you destroy seeds of self-respect. Simple, isn't it?

———✦———

Nothing does more to create a feeling of Self-respect than being a helping force in this world.

Commitment doesn't mean that the job,
the relationship, or the friendship has to last
forever. But while you are there, commit 100
percent. By doing so, the quality of your life
will also improve 100 percent.

Commit 100 percent…knowing that you
count. That's the magic duo!

NOT TO WORRY

Participating 100 percent eliminates boredom!

※

Action lessens fear. We get to sculpt our life instead of letting life sculpt us!

_____

One of the insidious qualities of fear is that it tends to permeate many areas of our lives.

———— ❈ ————

One of the glorious qualities about love is that it tends to permeate many areas of our lives.

NOT TO
WORRY

What is right? What is wrong? Who
knows? Do what feels right within
your heart.

Moving forward can be a very frightening,
yet powerful, act. In retreating, we come face
to face with the silent screams of helplessness.

Sometimes doors are closed for us, giving us no choice but to move forward. It's nice to think that our most difficult times are blessings in disguise!

The nature of growth is that it is always pulling us forward...despite how much we try to drag our feet.

NOT TO
WORRY

If we stopped dragging our feet…imagine
how much farther we'd go!

———❖———

**Life is about endings and beginnings.
The secret is knowing when to let go.**

We think of freedom as the unencumbered life, but it is really the unencumbered Self.

❖

The joy of becoming whole is always accompanied by tears. Every step toward a healthy body, mind, and Soul asks that we say good-bye to something familiar.

NOT TO WORRY

When the heart opens up, warm tears of both joy and sadness flow easily—**joy** from the feeling of oneness with all things that are human, **sadness** that we reject so much of what is human.

———— ❖ ————

Having it all really means accepting our choices and having no regrets about the road we didn't travel.

Have you noticed that if we don't learn our lessons, the Universe hands us many more opportunities for learning...until we get it right! Sometimes I wish the Universe wasn't so generous!

———❖———

You can't drink in tomorrow. But you can drink in today. How delicious!

NOT TO
WORRY

No matter what is going on in your life, you always have to remind yourself "I am a strong, loving, and worthy person." All situations in life flow harmoniously from this profound understanding of who you are.

IT'S ALL HAPPENING PERFECTLY

VII

IT'S ALL HAPPENING PERFECTLY!

SAY "YES!" TO LIFE! You can drop an awful lot of excess baggage if you learn to play with life instead of fighting it.

———————◆———————

Saying "NO!" means to block, to fight, to resist. Saying "YES!" means letting go of resistance and letting in possibilities for meaning and growth.

Whatever happens to you in life, just nod your head up and down instead of side to side. Just say "YES!" instead of "NO!"

Saying **"YES!"** means coming alive with possibility. It does not mean giving up; it means getting up and creating purpose in whatever life hands you. **That's power!**

IT'S ALL HAPPENING PERFECTLY!

Saying **"YES!"** is difficult sometimes. But don't say **"NO!"** to your difficulty in saying **"YES!"** That's self-punishment! It takes time to change old patterns. Allow yourself that time.

Saying **"YES!"** to Life is a miracle tool for dealing with your deepest darkest fears.

It's strange that we live in a culture that tells us not to be a "Pollyanna." What's wrong with feeling good about life despite what obstacles come your way? What's wrong with looking at the sun instead of gloom and doom? What's wrong with trying to see good in all things? **NOTHING IS WRONG WITH IT!** Why would you want to think any other way?!

IT'S ALL HAPPENING PERFECTLY!

Positive thinking offers you a power boost to help you handle whatever life hands you. Your "bad breaks" do not dominate your life…**your indomitable strength does.** In this lies an incredible sense of peace.

Positive thinking, in its most constructive form, does not deny the pain and suffering that exists in this world. To deny that they exist is irresponsible. We all need to be involved! And we have to approach our involvement with the positive attitude that something can be done.

IT'S ALL HAPPENING PERFECTLY!

Denial of pain is part of negative thinking. It says that pain is bad…something we need to avoid at all cost. How can something as human as pain be bad?

※

Acknowledgment of pain is part of positive thinking. It says that pain is part of life… something we ought to embrace, knowing that we will always get to the other side.

IT'S ALL HAPPENING PERFECTLY!

Hopelessness creates inactivity, and so does denial. Action is what is needed.

———— ❈ ————

Pain needn't wipe us out. It can strengthen us. We ultimately learn we can walk forward despite what hardships befall us.

IT'S ALL HAPPENING PERFECTLY!

Remember that...**even in the sunshine, one has to cry sometimes.**

———❖———

Throw away your picture of the way it's supposed to be. Only then can you have the freedom to enjoy the way it is.

IT'S ALL HAPPENING PERFECTLY!

_____

For all you "should-ers" out there, remember that the only way it "should" be at any given moment is exactly the way it is!

❖

When we send out negative energy, we attract negative energy. When we send out positive energy, we attract positive energy. And you doubt the value of positive thinking?!

IT'S ALL HAPPENING PERFECTLY!

A positive attitude is contagious. Spending time with a positive person makes us feel as though we can sprout wings and fly!

Being positive is much more realistic than being negative. Most of what we worry about never happens. But the more important issue is: **WHY BE MISERABLE WHEN YOU CAN BE HAPPY???**

IT'S ALL HAPPENING PERFECTLY!

There is no "realistic" or "unrealistic." There is only what we think about any given situation. We are capable of creating our own reality.

———❖———

All you have to do to change your world is change the way you think about it!

IT'S ALL HAPPENING PERFECTLY!

Weak words create a weak life. Strong
words create a strong life. Negative words
make us negative. Positive words make us
positive. Hateful words make us hateful.
Loving words make us loving. It's so
stunningly simple. You have the power
to choose.

Negativity has incredible staying power. But a few daily reminders of beauty, love, and joy are **much more** powerful, indeed.

There is always something to gain, never anything to lose, despite what choices we make or what actions we take in this world.

IT'S ALL HAPPENING
PERFECTLY!

_____

There is no such thing as a bad decision.
Each path is strewn with opportunities...
despite the outcome.

Many winners in life are those who have
been handed the worst life has to offer. So
you can't blame circumstances in your life for
holding you back! Sorry about that!

There are always gifts in a "bad" situation. Don't spend your time lamenting…spend your time finding the gifts!

HIGHER
AND HIGHER

VIII

HIGHER
AND HIGHER

If the path you're on isn't providing you a wonderful life, you're on the wrong path!

The path you are looking for is always **IN** and **UP**. When you are in touch with the highest part of who you are, your Higher Self, all is right with your world.

HIGHER
AND HIGHER

The Journey inward and upward is much
like the experience of climbing a mountain.
Sometimes the climb is tough. But each time
you stop to look around, the view becomes
more and more spectacular. And you are
propelled higher by the increasing beauty
you see.

———❖———

HIGHER
AND HIGHER

What do we find in the realm of the Higher Self? Creativity, intuition, trust, love, joy, inspiration, aspiration, caring, abundance, compassion, and all good things. Why would anyone resist?

———————❖———————

Too many of us seem to be searching for something "out there" to make our lives complete. What we are all really searching for is the divine essence that lives within.

———◆———

Modern society has been primarily concerned with body and mind. The Spiritual part, which encompasses the Higher Self, has somehow gotten lost in the shuffle.

HIGHER
AND HIGHER

If we want joy, satisfaction, and connection in our lives, body and mind is not enough. Spirit has to be included in the package.

Bringing the Spiritual into your life is easy. Ask your Higher Self what is the loving way of doing something, and then do it.

HIGHER
AND HIGHER

_____

The positive, loving, healing energy that flows from a heightened focus on Spirituality enriches every area of your life.

———❖———

Let me make it clear: Unless we consciously or unconsciously tap into the Spiritual part of who we are, we will experience perpetual discontent.

HIGHER
AND HIGHER

When we operate from the Higher Self, we feel centered and abundant, in fact, overflowing. When we experience this abundance, how can we ever feel afraid?

Learn the richness of solitude and quiet. That "still small voice" is yearning to be heard.

HIGHER
AND HIGHER

In the beginning, the quiet can be deafening.
It sounds something like, "Help!" But, soon
enough, we revel in the peace of it all.

———————❖———————

Once the voice within begins giving us
messages from our Higher Self instead of
hurtful messages from our Lower Self, we
really enjoy being alone.

HIGHER
AND HIGHER

Wouldn't you rather listen to the wisdom of your Higher Self than the hurtful chatter of your Lower Self?

---❖---

Constant activity in the outside world without the balance of inner activity, contributes to our loneliness. We end up separating ourselves from the very thing that gives us peace.

When we are in a state of upset, we know that we have strayed far from the abundance of the Higher Self. All we have to do to heal the upset is get back on the Spiritual path once again.

HIGHER
AND HIGHER

When the mind is cluttered, we only see
ourselves as fragmented and tired human
beings. When the mind is at peace, we
see ourselves floating in a sea of harmony.

———— ❖ ————

Any advice from our ego, or Lower Self, is
inherently a tool of separation rather than
one of connection. We are far better served
by tapping into our Higher Self for any
answers we may need.

Trust your intuition. It is the carrier of messages from the all-knowing place of power and love you hold inside. Whether you believe it or not, that place of power and wisdom is always there.

By learning to trust your intuition, "miracles" seem to happen. Intuitive thoughts are gifts from the Higher Self.

HIGHER
AND HIGHER

When in the center of your Higher Self, you always have the best seat! It's always your party!

The source of our love comes from within. No one out there is that source. It makes sense to go to the source.

When we trust ourselves and the "Grand Design," our life flows. When we lose that trust, we succeed only in driving ourselves crazy.

When we come from a place of trust, we see the exquisite order in all things.

HIGHER
AND HIGHER

When you can see yourself connected to something bigger than yourself, your sense of power becomes highly magnified and your fears are greatly diminished.

———❖———

If we don't make the Journey inward and upward, we will forever be alone. Once we find our Higher Self, we will never alone.

_____

When we connect with others from the Lower Self, it feels like a scary and potentially humiliating experience. When we connect with others from the Higher Self, it feels like an act of love.

———— ❈ ————

We need to make our Spiritual growth a lifelong commitment. Or as many lives as it takes!

HIGHER
AND HIGHER

It is in the Higher Self that we find the Heart
of Connection. From this transcendent place
it is possible to break down the walls of
separation and bring us into harmony with
ourselves and each other.

There's Paris, there's Rome, and a whole world out there to explore. But the Journey to the Spiritual part of who you are is the most fulfilling and exciting Journey you can ever take.

Spirituality is in the air, everywhere. So, delight in it as it washes over you like the long-awaited rain after a Summer's drought.

THERE'S ALWAYS MORE

IX

THERE'S ALWAYS
MORE

We come into this world as takers. We have to take, or we will die. But if we remain **only** takers, we will die another kind of death… death of the Spirit.

You are too important to deprive yourself and others of the power and love you hold within.

Sharing ourselves with others gives life meaning and purpose…a feeling of fulfillment and inner peace.

———❖———

There isn't a person alive who is not capable of greatly contributing to the well-being of this planet.

THERE'S ALWAYS MORE

Knowing that we can make a difference in this world is a great motivator. How can we know this and not be involved?

This is a "get-get-get" kind of world. Becoming a Giver requires that we let go of a lot of prior training, indeed.

Giving is about letting go of the crouched, withholding person and standing tall with outstretched arms.

———❖———

Lack is only in the mind. It's not about money. Some of the greatest givers I ever met were very money-poor.

THERE'S ALWAYS MORE

Giving away love is letting someone be who they are without trying to change them.

———❖———

Giving away love is trusting that someone can handle their own life without our intervention.

Giving away love is letting go and allowing someone to learn and grow without feeling our existence is threatened.

———— ❖ ————

Have you given away any love lately?

THERE'S ALWAYS
MORE

The question, **"What am I going to get?"** laces all our interactions with the fear of not getting…and ultimately, not getting enough.

———————❖———————

The question, **"What am I going to give?"** introduces a sense of outflow and abundance.

THERE'S ALWAYS MORE

Abundance is not about money or things; it is about love. When love is in your heart, you feel abundant…and that abundance runs over into everything and everyone around you.

To be the "giver" rather than the "getter" makes us feel more secure.

THERE'S ALWAYS MORE

Giving does not mean being a doormat for the hurtful people in your life! On the contrary, we need to walk away from people who treat us unkindly…**NOW!**

THERE'S NOTHING AS UNATTRACTIVE AS FOOTPRINTS ON THE FACE!

People who fear can't genuinely give. They have the erroneous assumption that there's not enough to go around. How silly!

When we give from a place of love, rather than from a place of expectation, there is an automatic payback of fulfillment.

THERE'S ALWAYS
MORE

If we are constantly expecting, we spend a great deal of our lives disappointed that the world isn't treating us right.

It's easy to give when you feel abundant, but you only feel abundant when you give. So what's the answer? Begin giving now!

When it comes to love, start giving it away instead of waiting for it to come to you.

———❖———

The way out of the "is this all there is" syndrome is to learn how to give.

WHEN WE HELP OTHER
PEOPLE, WE BECOME
MUCH BIGGER THAN WE
THOUGHT WE WERE.

THERE'S ALWAYS
MORE

Don't let an opportunity go by to thank
someone who has given you something…
anything at all.

———❖———

Open your eyes! Whether you presently
believe it or not, your life is already
abundant. Before you can accept abundance
in your life, you have to notice it!

THERE'S ALWAYS MORE

Life is huge! Rejoice about the sun, moon, flowers, and sky. Rejoice about the food you have to eat. Rejoice about the body that houses your spirit. Rejoice about the fact that you can be a positive force in the world around you. Rejoice about the love that is around you. If you want to be happy, commit to making your life one of rejoicing.

Daily, fill your diary with all the wonderful things you have to be grateful for. The doom and gloom, wish and want, will eventually fade into oblivion…which is where it belongs!

———◈———

There is so much you are not seeing that is already there. Look for the blessings, and you will notice them all over the place.

THERE'S ALWAYS MORE

Don't hold back. Give it away now! The supply of our love and caring is endless!

———❈———

It takes so little…just a little attention off the self, the opportunity to say to someone else, "Hi, I'm here. How can I help you on your Journey on this very strange planet?"

As we offer inspiration to others, we inspire ourselves. How's that for a "win-win" situation?

———❖———

The secret of a fear-less life is in figuring out what you can give, not what you can get. There is so much power in this kind of thinking, it staggers the imagination.

YOU ARE
THE WORLD

YOU ARE
THE WORLD

There is no easier way to affirm your inherent beauty than to live a life that matters.

———————❖———————

If you don't believe your life matters, act-as-if it does. Ask yourself, "If I were really important here, what would I be doing?" Then, do it. Eventually you will live in the knowledge that **your life really makes a difference.**

Understand that everything you do contributes to the pot of energy that defines the world. Look at your actions. What kind of contribution are you making?

―――――❖―――――

It is your involvement with the world that makes you feel you truly belong.

YOU ARE
THE WORLD

One simple act of caring and the whole world is transformed. Everyone is uplifted.

❈

To care is to automatically become at-one with another Soul.

Caring is a way of projecting our light. Acts of caring can be seen as light from the Soul.

———————————

We yearn for the delicious feelings that come from acts of caring. They make us feel useful, connected, and Spiritually whole. A life of emptiness could be transformed by a life of caring.

201

YOU ARE
THE WORLD

Our heart is healed only through loving,
caring, opening, sharing, helping, giving,
feeling, embracing, and warming the
world with our love.

We all have something to offer, whatever our
circumstances.

YOU ARE
THE WORLD

You and I have the power to begin the process of pulling our Society out of the realm of alienation and into a realm that feels much more like Home.

In a world of caring, there is no "over there." There is only all of us...everywhere ...one human family!

YOU ARE
THE WORLD

People with rich lives are people who care
about others, who are involved in projects
bigger than themselves, who appreciate
the gifts in all things, who reach out to help
others, who have respect for themselves, and
who get high on just being alive.

———❖———

As we walk into the freedom that human connection allows, something wonderful begins to happen. The numbness in our heart disappears, and feelings of empathy and caring come pouring in.

YOU ARE
THE WORLD

It feels so good to align with some higher purpose. We become bigger than we thought we were. We understand that our life has meaning. We grow up and move into true adult status where we know we have so much to give to this world.

YOU ARE
THE WORLD

When we all pull together in a time of crisis, we rise above the level of our individual differences, and we stop competing.
It is then that we understand what "one human family" is all about.

YOU ARE
THE WORLD

We experience the Higher Self during those
times when we realize that "we are all in it
together." For those brief moments in time,
the externals of our life, which usually
seem so important, now seem petty and
unimportant as we touch a more noble
place within.

YOU ARE
THE WORLD

The road to connection is clear. It begins inside and radiates out to everyone around us in an ever-growing beam of light.

———— ❖ ————

As long as we are showering love into the world, we will never be bored. There's too much to do!

YOU ARE
THE WORLD

Liberation, for both men and women, is really about letting our light shine through. As we become the best that we can be, we understand the true meaning of being free.

———— ❖ ————

Who you are is someone who has the power within to create a Heaven on earth for yourself and to radiate a piece of that Heaven out to everyone whose life touches yours.

210

YOU ARE
THE WORLD

———————————

The whole of the human species is crying out
for love. If we all take the time to look into
our hearts, we will ultimately feel complete
and connected…within ourselves and as part
of the human family.

———————————

———————————

WHEREVER YOUR JOURNEY TAKES YOU, COMMIT TO LIVING EACH DAY OF YOUR LIFE AS A SOURCE OF POWER AND LOVE. IN THIS LIES YOUR *GUARANTEE* OF A LIFE FILLED WITH JOY AND SATISFACTION!

———————— ❖ ————————

ABOUT THE AUTHOR

SUSAN JEFFERS, PH.D., has helped millions of people overcome their fears and move forward in life with confidence and love. She is also one of the leading authorities on creating healthy relationships. Dr. Jeffers is the author of the bestselling books, *Feel the Fear and Do It Anyway, Dare to Connect, Opening Our Hearts to Men,* and *The Journey from Lost to Found,* plus her "FEAR-LESS SERIES" of affirmation books and tapes *(Inner Talk for Peace of Mind, Inner Talk for a Confident Day,* and *Inner Talk for a Love That Works)*. She has also created many audiocassettes on fear, relationships, and personal growth. As well as being a popular workshop leader and public speaker, she has been a guest on many radio and television shows, including *Oprah, Sally Jessy Raphael, Montel Williams,* and *Jenny Jones.*

We hope you enjoyed this Hay House book. If you would like to receive a free catalog featuring additional Hay House books and products, or if you would like information about the Hay Foundation, please write to:

Hay House, Inc.
1154 E. Dominguez St.
P.O. Box 6204
Carson, CA 90749-6204

or call:

(800) 654-5126